TextMate How-To

Over 20 fast and furious timesaving recipes for
using TextMate efficiently and effectively

Chris Mears

BIRMINGHAM - MUMBAI

TextMate How-To

First published: October 2012

Production Reference: 1191012

Published by Packt Publishing Ltd.
Livery Place
35 Livery Street
Birmingham B3 2PB, UK.

ISBN 978-1-84969-398-1

www.packtpub.com

Credits

Author

Chris Mears

Reviewers

Shifra Pride Raffel

Simone Silvestroni

Acquisition Editor

Kartikey Pandey

Commissioning Editor

Priyanka Shah

Technical Editor

Dominic Pereira

Copy Editor

Aditya Nair

Project Coordinator

Shraddha Bagadia

Proofreader

Aaron Nash

Production Coordinator

Prachali Bhiwandkar

Cover Work

Prachali Bhiwandkar

Cover Work

Conidon Miranda

About the Author

Chris Mears lives in San Francisco and is the lead web developer at Canned Banners, a startup he co-founded. Though he considers himself a generalist when it comes to technology, he finds true passion developing for the Web. When he's not thinking and dreaming about code, he enjoys going to concerts, practicing on his guitar, homebrewing beer, and tea snobbery. This is his first book.

I'd like to thank Anna for her support and the proofreading she performed throughout the writing of this book. I'd like to thank my friends and family (and the family of my friends), who have given me words of encouragement. Last, but certainly not least, I'd like to thank my friend and past colleague, Shifra, for being a great technical editor and also fixing all of my grammatical mistakes.

About the Reviewers

Shifra Pride Raffel is a Java developer in the Bay Area. She has been developing software for 14 years, has worked as an Agile software development process consultant for Pivotal Labs, and currently works for MSCI in Berkeley (her technical reviewing of this book reflected only her opinion and not that of MSCI).

Simone Silvestroni is a multidisciplinary designer and developer, working in web UI for 12 years. He is based in Milan and London.

Starting as a print designer and desktop publisher in 1993, he crossed through different creative and technical fields closely related to web designing and coding. His key skill is turning raw sketched ideas into live interfaces, and studying and modifying them through user tests while always keeping a keen eye on accessibility and typography.

Simone is also a graduated musician, a sound designer, and a bassist.

He worked for the biggest publishing company in Italy (RCS) for several years, joined a startup in February 2000, and became a team leader of the sound and web designing team and remained so until the end of 2004, working on the prototype for a PlayStation 2 platform game.

He co-founded his own company in 2004 and co-ran it until the end of 2007, when he joined a full-service web agency and led the user experience team for four years. After relocating to London, UK, he joined a leading online gaming company, eventually co-founding his new startup, UI Farm Ltd, a small UI and UX agency focused on responsive design and riding the incoming mobile wave.

www.PacktPub.com

Support files, eBooks, discount offers and more

You might want to visit www.PacktPub.com for support files and downloads related to your book.

Did you know that Packt offers eBook versions of every book published, with PDF and ePub files available? You can upgrade to the eBook version at www.PacktPub.com and as a print book customer, you are entitled to a discount on the eBook copy. Get in touch with us at service@packtpub.com for more details.

At www.PacktPub.com, you can also read a collection of free technical articles, sign up for a range of free newsletters and receive exclusive discounts and offers on Packt books and eBooks.

http://PacktLib.PacktPub.com

Do you need instant solutions to your IT questions? PacktLib is Packt's online digital book library. Here, you can access, read and search across Packt's entire library of books.

Why Subscribe?

- ► Fully searchable across every book published by Packt
- ► Copy and paste, print and bookmark content
- ► On demand and accessible via web browser

Free Access for Packt account holders

If you have an account with Packt at www.PacktPub.com, you can use this to access PacktLib today and view nine entirely free books. Simply use your login credentials for immediate access.

Table of Contents

Preface

TextMate is a highly extensible Mac OS X GUI text editor that has gained quite a bit of developer notoriety through the years. Created in 2004 by Allan Odgaard, TextMate 1 started out as a simple editor. By 2006, when TextMate 1.5 was released, it won the Apple Design Award for Best Developer Tool, and has gained a vast community backing.

In August 2012, TextMate 2 was released under GNU General Public License and its source code is available at Github. However, this guide will cover the most popular version of the software, TextMate 1.5.

The goal of this book is to provide its readers a succinct set of recipes to become familiar with TextMate's most useful features and bundles, in order to hit the ground running and code more quickly and efficiently.

What this book covers

Configuring TextMate, guides you through the most common configuration topics so you can customize your TextMate experience quickly.

Installing themes, covers downloading and installing themes to personalize your document window and code coloring.

Quickly navigating to text, demonstrates how to navigate the text and document quickly and easily with keyboard shortcuts.

Converting text, provides an overview of the most common built-in text conversions that will speed up your editing.

Moving and aligning text, walks you through how to move and align text in your document.

Manipulating multiple lines and columns of text, provides a very useful recipe for editing multiple lines of text at the same time.

Finding and replacing text, demonstrates TextMate's extremely powerful Find and Replace functionality.

Folding, teaches you how to use Folding to organize code.

Bookmarking, walks you through using bookmarks to quickly navigate to important lines.

Creating projects, covers creating and saving projects through various methods, including opening directories, dragging-and-dropping, and using the command line.

Utilizing tabs, runs you through the various ways to navigate tabs, mostly via keyboard shortcuts.

Traversing files, teaches you how to quickly and easily open files within a project without reaching for the mouse.

Finding text in a project, describes another way to find text, this time searching through your entire project. This task will also include some tips on how to speed up your search and even cover some caveats for larger projects.

Installing bundles with GetBundles, covers the finding and installation of bundles with GetBundles, which is a bundle that allows you to install other publicly available bundles.

Learning and loving bundles, quickly describes the use of bundles, including the beauty of tab completions and how to easily find the bundle item you're looking for along with the tab completion abbreviation or the keyboard shortcut.

Making a TODO list, utilizes the official TextMate TODO bundle to display a to-do list compiled directly from your project using common comment keywords such as TODO, FIXME, CHANGED, and RADAR.

Becoming a Zen Coding master, demonstrates the Zen Coding philosophy and use of the most common bundle items.

Blogging more efficiently, describes how to use a few of the more useful blogging bundles (Blogging and Hyperlink Helper) in order to work more efficiently when offline.

Markdown and Textile, covers both text formats and describes why you may want to use one over the other depending on your project.

Using macros, provides an overview on how to record and subsequently execute macros in your document to speed up common tasks.

Executing shell commands, demonstrates how to run shell commands directly from the current document.

What you need for this book

This How-To guide is for users with a basic understanding of TextMate. You should have TextMate 1.5.x installed.

Who this book is for

This book is geared toward beginner and intermediate web developers and designers who want to speed up their coding. Though TextMate can also work very well as a plain text editor, some experience with a programming or scripting language, whether it's HTML, CSS, PHP, or Ruby, is helpful to understand the depth to some of the examples provided.

Conventions

In this book, you will find a number of styles of text that distinguish between different kinds of information. Here are some examples of these styles, and an explanation of their meaning.

Code words in text are shown as follows: "The `.tmbundle` file will open as a project."

Any command-line input or output is written as follows:

```
cd ~/Library/Application\ Support/TextMate/Bundles.
```

New terms and **important words** are shown in bold. Words that you see on the screen, in menus or dialog boxes for example, appear in the text like this: "clicking the **Next** button moves you to the next screen".

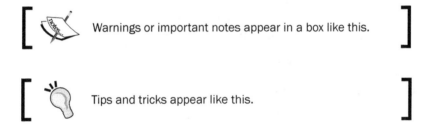

Warnings or important notes appear in a box like this.

Tips and tricks appear like this.

Reader feedback

Feedback from our readers is always welcome. Let us know what you think about this book—what you liked or may have disliked. Reader feedback is important for us to develop titles that you really get the most out of.

To send us general feedback, simply send an e-mail to feedback@packtpub.com, and mention the book title via the subject of your message.

If there is a book that you need and would like to see us publish, please send us a note in the **SUGGEST A TITLE** form on www.packtpub.com or e-mail suggest@packtpub.com.

If there is a topic that you have expertise in and you are interested in either writing or contributing to a book, see our author guide on www.packtpub.com/authors.

Customer support

Now that you are the proud owner of a Packt book, we have a number of things to help you to get the most from your purchase.

Errata

Although we have taken every care to ensure the accuracy of our content, mistakes do happen. If you find a mistake in one of our books—maybe a mistake in the text or the code—we would be grateful if you would report this to us. By doing so, you can save other readers from frustration and help us improve subsequent versions of this book. If you find any errata, please report them by visiting http://www.packtpub.com/support, selecting your book, clicking on the **errata submission form** link, and entering the details of your errata. Once your errata are verified, your submission will be accepted and the errata will be uploaded on our website, or added to any list of existing errata, under the Errata section of that title. Any existing errata can be viewed by selecting your title from http://www.packtpub.com/support.

Piracy

Piracy of copyright material on the Internet is an ongoing problem across all media. At Packt, we take the protection of our copyright and licenses very seriously. If you come across any illegal copies of our works, in any form, on the Internet, please provide us with the location address or website name immediately so that we can pursue a remedy.

Please contact us at copyright@packtpub.com with a link to the suspected pirated material.

We appreciate your help in protecting our authors, and our ability to bring you valuable content.

Questions

You can contact us at questions@packtpub.com if you are having a problem with any aspect of the book, and we will do our best to address it.

TextMate How-To

TextMate is an extremely powerful and highly extensible GUI text editor for Mac OS X. Since its release in 2004, it has garnered a huge community of supporters, won awards, and is considered one of the best coding platforms on the Mac for web developers, designers, and serious programmers. This How-To will guide you through the best techniques to hit the ground running and code like a professional.

Configuring TextMate (Must know)

This task will quickly go through some of the more helpful configuration options, including some **Preference** and **View** settings. Note that these settings are purely my preferences and are only meant to show where to find them. You should set up TextMate however you feel comfortable, and based upon your particular project.

How to do it...

To configure **Line Numbers**:

1. From the menu, select **View | Gutter | Line Numbers** (*Option + Command + L*) to toggle them on and off.

To configure **Soft Tabs**:

1. From the status bar, located at the bottom of the document window, click on the **Tab Size** pop-up menu, and select **Soft Tabs**.
2. From the same pop-up menu, select the desired tab size (usually 2 or 4).

To configure **Soft Wrap**:

1. From the menu, select **View** | **Soft Wrap** (*Option + Command + W*).

2. To choose the width of the wrap, from the menu select **View** | **Wrap Column**. Selecting **Use Window Frame** will change the wrap width depending on the overall width of the document window.

To configure the **Show Invisibles** option:

1. From the menu, select **View** | **Show Invisibles** (*Option + Command + I*). Two examples are shown in the following screenshot:

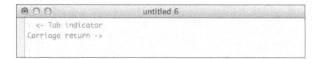

To configure **Check Spelling as You Type**:

1. From the menu, select **Edit** | **Spelling** | **Check Spelling as You Type** (*Option + Command + ;*).

Selecting **Highlight current line, Show right margin indicator**, and **Highlight right margin**:

1. From the menu, select **TextMate** | **Preferences** (*Command + ,*).

2. In **Preferences**, under the **General** tab, check **Highlight current line, Show right margin indicator**, and **Highlight right margin**.

```
126    /*
127    Typography
128
129
130    abbr[title] {
131        border-bottom: 1px dotted;
132    }
133
134    b,
135    strong {
136        font-weight: bold;
137    }
138
139    blockquote {
140        margin: 1em 40px;
141    }
142
143    dfn {
144        font-style: italic;
145    }
146
147    hr {
148        display: block;
149        height: 1px;
150        border: 0;
151        border-top: 1px solid #ccc;
152        margin: 1em 0;
153        padding: 0;
154    }
155
Line: 136   Column: 22    CSS         Soft Tabs:  2    CSS: b, strong
```

How it works...

Now, let's go through why you may want to use these settings:

- **Line Numbers**: They are helpful to establish where you are in a document. If you'd rather have fewer margin distractions, then you can also determine your cursor's current line and column position in the status bar at the bottom of the document window.

- **Soft Tabs**: Soft tabs versus hard tabs are somewhat controversial (do a Google search and you'll see). You should really use what you're most comfortable with or what conforms to the project or document style rules.

- **Soft Wrap**: This will wrap lines based on your margin column width settings. If this is not set and there's a line that goes beyond the document window's view, scrolling will be necessary to view the rest of the line.

- **Show Invisibles**: This will show tabs and line returns. Sometimes, this is helpful for troubleshooting some oddities in your document, such as why a tab isn't lining up properly. They are also helpful to get a complete picture of your code. However, if you would rather not have the clutter, it's perfectly reasonable to turn this setting off.

- **Check Spelling as You Type**: This will provide the familiar wiggly red line under misspelled words. Right-clicking on the words will provide alternate word options. It's only necessary when composing written words, but TextMate is smart enough to determine when you're writing code and won't try to spell check everything.

- **Highlight current line**: This will provide a horizontal highlight to indicate in which line your cursor is located. The **right margin indicator** option will provide a vertical line to indicate the right margin, and the **Highlight right margin** option will highlight the right margin. These visual indicators, or **ornaments**, will help show you where your cursor is in the document, as well as where the right margin is located. Knowing where the right margin is can be helpful for keeping code readable and well styled. For example, if some of your fellow coders are accessing the files via shell editors (that is, vim, emacs, nano, and so on), they may have limited document width based on their particular terminal program.

There's more...

Included with the TextMate application is a command-line tool, which can be used in Terminal to open files. In addition, it's quite important to learn the keyboard shortcuts, which will help you do things quickly and efficiently. However, in order to learn the shortcuts, it is vital to learn what the keyboard symbols look like.

Enhanced Terminal Usage

When you run TextMate for the first time, you will be prompted to install the shell command `mate`. Installing this tool will allow you to open files into TextMate from Terminal, for example, `mate example.html` or `mate project/`. There is more on opening files in the *Traversing files* recipe.

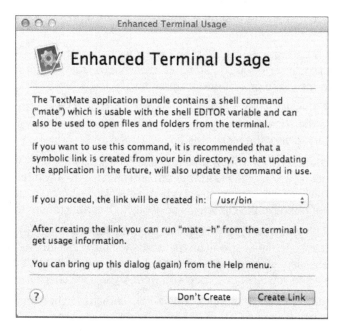

You can open the install dialog at any time from the menu; select **Help | Terminal Usage**.

Keyboard shortcuts

TextMate is most powerful when you use keyboard shortcuts as opposed to reaching for the mouse and selecting menu items. This How-To will try to provide the keyboard shortcuts for as many of the functions as possible.

Installing themes (Must know)

Though it doesn't do much for the actual usage of the application, themes and code coloring will help with understanding and interpretation of any text or code you'll be dealing with. TextMate comes with a number of themes already installed (accessible via **Preferences**), but if you can't find one that suits your particular tastes, this task will go through downloading and installing a theme, specifically the popular and freely available **RailsCasts** theme.

Getting ready

Download the ZIP file at `https://github.com/ryanb/textmate-themes`. This is shown in the following screenshot:

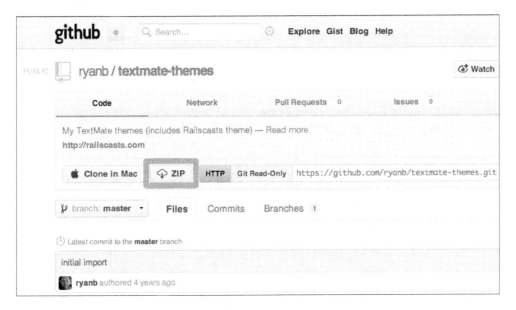

How to do it...

Once the ZIP file is downloaded, extract it and double-click on the theme files which have the `.tmTheme` extension to install and switch to the theme. The theme files are shown in the following screenshot:

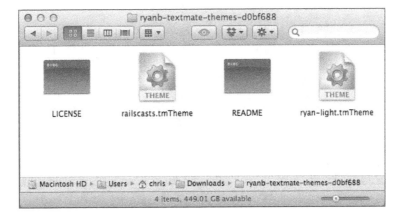

How it works...

Made famous by Ryan Bates' screencasts (http://www.railscasts.com), RailsCasts is a great and aesthetically pleasing theme that can be used for a number of languages, including PHP, Ruby, HTML, and JavaScript.

You will notice that the RailsCasts theme ZIP file contains two versions. The one labeled **ryan-light.tmTheme** has a white background. The original has a dark background and is also the version used for most of the screenshots in this guide. Whichever you choose to use is purely your preference, but there is no harm in installing and trying both.

You can switch themes by going to **File** | **Preferences** (*Command + ,*) and selecting the **Fonts & Colors** tab, as shown in the following screenshot:

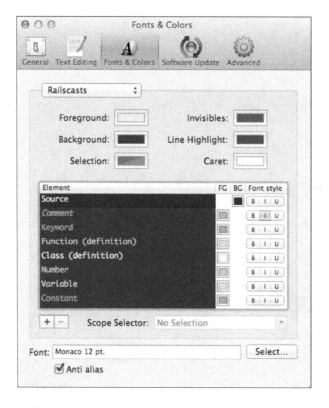

There's more...

In case the included or RailsCasts theme doesn't adhere to your particular tastes, there are many other popular themes available.

Solarized theme

Another freely available theme is called **Solarized**, and can be found at `https://github.com/deplorableword/textmate-solarized`. The Solarized theme is stated to be specifically useful on calibrated and non-calibrated displays alike, as well as in a variety of lighting conditions. Since the theme consists of a simple color palette, it's easily translatable to terminal emulations and therefore highly versatile between applications.

You can find out more about the Solarized theme, including themes for additional applications, at `http://ethanschoonover.com/solarized`.

More themes!

There are many more themes available on the **Macromates** wiki:

`http://wiki.macromates.com/Themes/UserSubmittedThemes`

Quickly navigating to text (Must know)

This task will show you how to navigate the document and text, in most cases without reaching for the mouse or track pad.

How to do it...

The two available options to quickly navigate to the text are as follows:

▸ **Go to Line...** will move your cursor to the specified line number. From the menu, select **Navigation | Go to Line...** (*Command + L*).

▸ **Go to Symbol...** will move your cursor to the beginning of a function, method, or other symbol. From the menu, select **Navigation | Go to Symbol...** (*Shift + Command + T*).

How it works...

Go to Line... (*Command + L*) is very useful for situations where you know the precise line you want to edit. For example, when you're debugging some code and the error message code gives the problem line number.

Go to Symbol... (*Shift + Command + T*) is mainly used for programming languages such as JavaScript and PHP, where functions or methods are defined in the document. When this is invoked, a window will appear with the names of the functions or methods available, as shown in the following screenshot:

Start entering the method name and it will match and filter the list based on what you enter. **Go to Symbol...** (*Shift + Command + T*) is extremely helpful for long documents of code where scrolling and navigating line by line is unreasonable.

You can also open the function pop up in the status menu (located at the bottom of the document window) to display all of the functions or methods in your document. This is shown in the following screenshot:

```
919
920    /* MODAL PLUGIN DEFINITION
921    * ============================= */
922
923    $.fn.modal = function (option) {
924        return this.each(function () {
925            var $this = $(this)
926              , data = $this.data('modal')
927              , options = $.extend({}, $.fn.modal.defaul
       option)
928            if (!data) $this.data('modal', (data = new M
929            if (typeof option == 'string') data[option](
930            else if (options.show) data.show()
931        })
932    }
```

```
keydown
clearMenus
getParent
dropdown
Dropdown
Modal
toggle
show
hide
enforceFocus
escape
hideWithTransition
hideModal
removeBackdrop
backdrop
modal
Modal
Tooltip
init
getOptions
enter
leave
show
setContent
hide
removeWithAnimation
fixTitle
```

Line: 928   Column: 1   jQuery (JavaScript)   Soft Tabs: 4   ✓ Modal

There's more...

Along with the quick navigation shortcuts, there are also ways to move the cursor and scroll the document easily without using the mouse.

Cursor movement

The following keyboard shortcuts will move your cursor:

Shortcut	Description
Shift + F	One character forward.
Shift + B	One character backward.
Shift + P	Up one line.
Shift + N	Down one line.
Shift + A	Beginning of line.
Shift + E	End of line.
Option + right arrow	Right one word (Mac convention).
Option + left arrow	Left one word (Mac convention).

Note that the first four movements can be accomplished by using the arrow keys, but sometimes it's faster to keep your fingers on the keyboard home row.

Scrolling the document without moving the cursor

In the situation where you want to take a peek within the document without moving the cursor, you can use the keyboard shortcut *Command + Option + Control* plus the arrow keys. For example, to scroll up, you would press *Command + Option + Control +* up arrow. Your cursor will stay put and you can go back to it by using the *Command + J* (that is, select **Edit | Find | Jump to Selection**) keyboard shortcut.

Converting text (Must know)

This task will demonstrate how to convert text in various ways.

How to do it...

TextMate provides the following text conversions:

- ▶ **Uppercase**: This will convert the entire selected text to uppercase letters. From the menu, select **Text | Convert | to Uppercase** (*Control + U*).

- ▶ **Lowercase**: This will convert the entire selected text to lowercase letters. From the menu, select **Text | Convert | to Lowercase** (*Control + Shift + U*).

- ▶ **Title case**: This will convert the first letter of each word in the selection to uppercase. From the menu, select **Text | Convert | to Title case** (*Option + Control + U*).

- ▶ **Opposite case**: This will swap the case of each letter of the selection (for example, lowercase will become uppercase and uppercase will become lowercase). From the menu, select **Text | Convert | to Opposite case** (*Control + G*).

- ▶ **Spaces to Tabs**: This will convert spaces to tabs (as defined in Tab Size). From the menu, select **Text | Convert | Spaces to Tabs**.

- ▶ **Tabs to Spaces**: This will convert tabs to spaces (as defined in Tab Size). From the menu, select **Text | Convert | Tabs to Spaces**.

- ▶ **Transpose**: This will output the selection backwards. From the menu, select **Text | Convert | Transpose** (*Control + T*).

How it works...

Most of these conversions should be self-explanatory. Some text conversions are shown in the following screenshot:

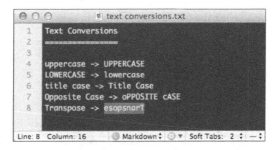

Tabs to Spaces (or **Spaces to Tabs**) is helpful if you decide later on to change to or from **Soft Tabs**. It's also useful if you want to play a practical joke on a colleague who is vehemently against either soft or hard tabs.

Moving and aligning text (Should know)

This task will show you how to move text around, whether you want to move a selection of text up, down, or align it.

How to do it...

The different options used to move and align text are as follows:

- ▸ Moving a selection up a line will insert the selected text into the previous line. From the menu, select **Text | Move Selection | Line Up** (*Command* + *Control* + up arrow).

- ▸ Moving a selection down a line will insert the selected text into the next line. From the menu, select **Text | Move Selection | Line Down** (*Command* + *Control* + down arrow).

- ▸ Left aligning will align text to the left. From the menu, select **Text | Align | Left**.

- ▸ Right aligning will align text to the right margin based on the **Wrap Column** setting. From the menu, select **Text | Align | Right**.

- ▸ Center aligning will center text using the **Wrap Column** setting as a guide. From the menu, select **Text | Align | Center**.

- ▸ Justifying will space out the text evenly using the **Wrap Column** setting as a guide. From the menu, select **Text | Align | Justify**.

How it works...

Moving selections: When you are moving a selection of text, it is just as if you are dragging the text around with your mouse cursor (see *Moving text with the mouse/track pad* in the *There's more...* section). Don't be afraid. As you'll see in the following screenshot, it will not overwrite the line you are moving your selection to:

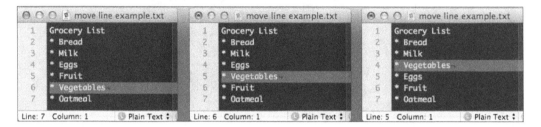

Aligning text: An important thing to note is that the alignment is based on the **Wrap Column** size (select **View | Wrap Column**).

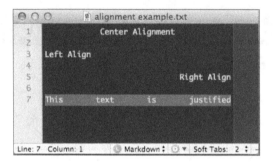

There's more...

Since TextMate is a full-featured GUI text editor, you may also move text with the mouse or track pad. Plus, we'll look at a tip for moving entire lines up or down.

Moving text with the mouse/track pad

You can also move the text around by clicking and dragging a selection with your mouse or track pad, just like most other word processors. However, keeping your hands on the keyboard is faster and reduces repetitive strain (that is, carpal tunnel syndrome), and is typically preferred by hardcore coders.

Tip for moving entire lines of text

You can also move the entire line with the cursor, not by making a selection, but rather by invoking **Line Up** (*Command* + *Control* + up arrow) or **Line Down** (*Command* + *Control* + down arrow). However, notice that your cursor will stay positioned on the previous line. Therefore, you may prefer to select the line (*Command* + *Shift* + *L*) and then move it around as you please.

Manipulating multiple lines and columns of text (Should know)

This is a more advanced task that will show how to select and edit multiple lines and columns of text.

Getting ready

Since this task is most useful with a list or multiple columns of text, you'll want to start out with something like the following:

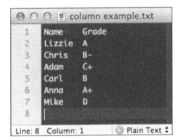

How to do it...

The steps to manipulate multiple lines and multiple columns of text are as follows:

1. Make a selection, ending the selection after the final character of the last row, as shown in the following screenshot:

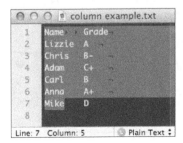

2. Switch to **Column Selection** by pressing the **Option** key, or from the menu, select **Edit | Change to Column Selection**:

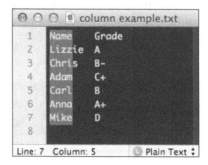

3. Edit the selection by holding down the *Shift* key and moving with the arrow keys. In this case, hold *Shift* and tap the right arrow key once to complete the full column selection:

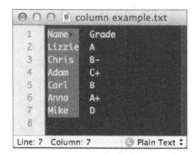

4. While the column is selected, you can move it by selecting **Text | Move Selection | Column Left** (*Command + Control* + left arrow) or by selecting **Text | Move Selection | Column Right** (*Command + Control* + right arrow).

5. To edit all of the lines in a selection, make your selection, and from the menu, select **Text | Edit Each Line in Selection** (*Command + Option + A*). Once this is done, start typing and each line will be changed:

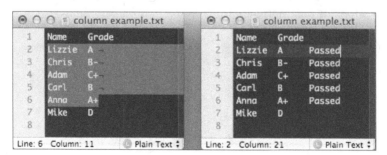

How it works...

Though the column manipulation is mainly used for data organization, the **Edit all lines in a selection** option has some very practical use cases for editing code. For example, if you have a list of items in HTML but don't want to copy and paste list item tags (that is, `<li>`) for each line, you can use the following set of keystrokes to quickly surround all of the items in `<li>` tags.

Select all of the lines, press *Command + Option + A*, and start typing the opening tag (`<li>`), followed by *Command* + right arrow (to move to the end of the line), and type the closing tag (`</li>`):

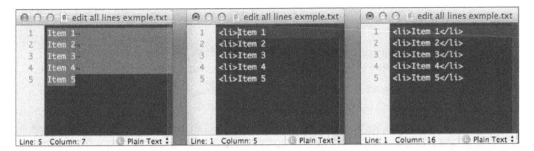

Finding and replacing text (Must know)

This task will show you how to find text in the document using a string or a regular expression, as well as replace the text you find.

How to do it...

The different **Find** options are explained as follows:

▶ The **Find** option will search for any occurrence of a specified string. From the menu, select **Edit | Find | Find...** (*Command + F*). For finding a normal string, uncheck the **Regular expression** checkbox:

- The **Find** option with the **Regular expression** checkbox checked will search for any occurrence using regular expressions. To do this, select **Edit | Find | Find...**:

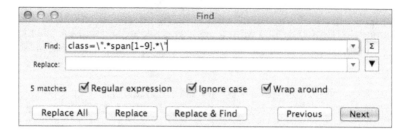

- The **Find Next** option will search for the next occurrence. From the menu, select **Edit | Find | Find Next** (*Command + G*).

- The **Find Previous** option will search for the previous occurrence. From the menu, select **Edit | Find | Find Previous** (*Command + Shift + G*).

- The **Use Selection for Find** option will search for the selected text. From the menu, select **Edit | Find | Use Selection for Find** (*Command + E*).

- The **Replace** text functionality is included in the **Find** dialog box (select **Edit | Find | Find...** or *Command + F*). You can use **Replace**, **Replace All**, or **Replace & Find**, which are described in more detail in the *How it works...* section.

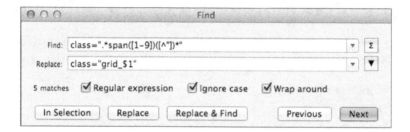

How it works...

The **Find** dialog box has some very helpful options. These are as follows:

- **Ignore case** will perform a find irrespective of case.

- **Replace** will replace the currently selected find occurrence.

- **Replace All** will replace all find occurrences in the document.

- **Replace & Find** is useful to test out your find occurrences before using **Replace All** and is also useful when you're not quite certain if you want to replace everything.

- The **Σ** button will output the number of occurrences of the find string or regular expression. This is helpful to do before a full replacement. Also, you can gauge the extent of the upcoming changes and make edits to your find text, if needed.

There's more...

There are some extended features of the find functionality that are useful if you do a lot of searching or if you need to find and/or replace multiple lines.

Find and Replace history

In case you want to repeat a past **Find and Replace** search, there's a history drop-down you can use by clicking on the downward-facing triangle next to the input boxes.

Expanded Find and Replace

If you need some more room to fully view your Find and Replace strings or regular expressions, you can click on the downward-facing triangle underneath the **Σ** button:

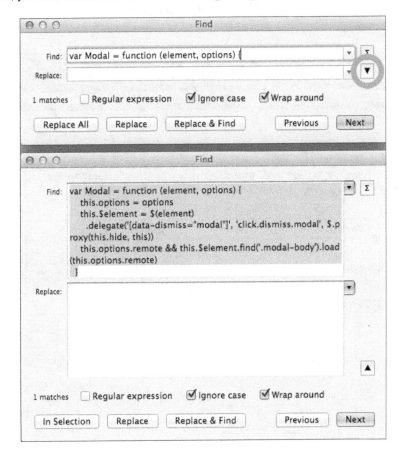

Also, if you need to insert a literal tab or return, hold down the *Option* key while pressing *Tab* or *return*.

Folding (Should know)

Folding is a great way to organize your code as well as hide lines in order to focus on the current task at hand.

Getting ready

To use folding, you'll need to make sure it's enabled. You can toggle it by going to **View | Gutter | Foldings** from the menu.

How to do it...

Folding actually happens automatically as long as you have the proper language selected via the status bar pop-up:

Shortcut	Description
F1	Fold current block.
Option + Command + 0	Fold **All Levels** toggle.
Option + Command + 1–Option + Command + 9	Fold at level (1-9).

How it works...

As with most of TextMate's functions, learning the keyboard shortcuts for folding is key to working with your document.

But, you can also use the mouse and click the arrows to fold the code, as shown in the following screenshot:

```
25
26    /* MODAL CLASS DEFINITION
27     * ========================= */
28
29    var Modal = function (content, options) {
30        this.options = options
31        this.$element = $(content)
32            .delegate('[data-dismiss="modal"]', 'click.dismiss.modal',
      $.proxy(this.hide, this))
33    }
34
35    Modal.prototype = {
36
37        constructor: Modal
38
39      , toggle: function () {...
162   }
163
164   function removeBackdrop() {...
168
169   function escape() {...
179
```

There's more...

It's important that your document is set to the correct language for folding and other features, such as bundle snippets and shortcuts, to work properly. You can quickly change languages using keyboard shortcuts.

Language keyboard shortcuts

Notice the keyboard shortcuts next to the language selection pop-up. These can be very helpful in quickly switching languages (for example, between HTML and PHP or HTML and JavaScript).

Sometimes the document is coded in two languages (for example, HTML and PHP) and you need certain bundle functionality, depending on the setting (bundles will be discussed further in the *Bundles* recipe).

Bookmarking (Should know)

Bookmarking is a great way to save a line of code so that you can navigate back to it later or cycle among all of your bookmarks.

How to do it...

You can use the following methods to bookmark a line:

- ▸ From the menu, select **Navigation | Add Bookmark and Navigation | Remove Bookmark**.
- ▸ The keyboard shortcut *Command + F2*

▶ Click on the gutter next to the line in order to toggle the bookmark:

```
918
919
920  /* MODAL PLUGIN DEFINITION
921  * ============================== */
922
923  $.fn.modal = function (option) {
924      return this.each(function () {
925          var $this = $(this)
926          , data = $this.data('modal')
927          , options = $.extend({}, $.fn.modal.defaults, $this.data(), typeof
     option == 'object' && option)
928          if (!data) $this.data('modal', (data = new Modal(this, options)))
929          if (typeof option == 'string') data[option]()
930          else if (options.show) data.show()
931      })
932  }
933
934  $.fn.modal.defaults = {
935      backdrop: true
936      , keyboard: true
937      , show: true
938  }
939
940  $.fn.modal.Constructor = Modal
941
942
943  /* MODAL DATA-API
```

Line: 928   Column: 1   jQuery (JavaScript)   Soft Tabs: 4   Modal

How it works...

A star indicator in the gutter signifies when a line has been bookmarked.

▶ The **Next Bookmark** option is used to go to the next bookmark in the document. From the menu, select **Navigation | Next Bookmark** (*F2*).

▶ The **Previous Bookmark** option is used to go the previous bookmark in the document. From the menu, select **Navigation | Previous Bookmark** (*Shift + F2*).

Creating projects (Must know)

This task will cover creating and saving projects through various methods, including opening directories, drag-and-drop, and by using the command line.

Getting ready

If you would like to use the drag-and-drop to dock method, you will need to copy the TextMate application to the dock.

If you would like to use the command-line method, you will need to install the `mate` command-line executable, which you are prompted to do during the first run of TextMate. You may also install it from the **File** menu (select **Help | Terminal Usage...**) at any time. See the *Configuring TextMate* section explained earlier in the chapter, for more information.

How to do it...

Let's cover the typical ways to create projects in TextMate:

- Create a new project through the menu (select **File | New Project**) or with the keyboard shortcut (*Command + Control + N*). You can then add files to it by dragging and dropping from the **Finder** or by adding existing files from the **Project Drawer** toolbar, as shown in the following screenshot:

- Opening a folder or multiple files will also create a project. You can do this from the menu by selecting **File | Open** (*Command + O*).

- Dragging and dropping a folder or multiple files to a TextMate dock item will open those files into a new project. This is shown in the following screenshot:

- Command line is also available if you're comfortable in the Terminal. You can create new projects via the `mate` shell command. Some examples are as follows:

```
mate howto.txt notes.txt   # Open multiple files
mate textmate-howto/       # Open a folder
mate .                     # Open current directory
```

How it works...

Projects allow you to quickly work with multiple files. Once created, you can quickly search for and open files (see the *Traversing Files* section), create new files, organize files into groups, create project-specific shell variables, and more.

Once you open a project, you can easily save it by selecting **File | Save Project** (*Command + Control + S*) or by selecting **File | Save Project As...** (*Command + Control + Shift + S*). The latter will allow you to rename a previously saved project.

There's more...

Let's cover how to exclude files or folders from your projects, as well as why you may want to do so.

Excluding files

Sometimes excluding files will speed up search time, for example, if your project includes long logfiles with the extension `.log`. Unfortunately, the process to exclude files requires knowledge of regular expressions, which is a bit out of the scope of this book.

However, you can find where to exclude files by going to **File | Preferences** (*Command + ,*), navigating to the **Advanced** tab, and selecting the **Folder References** section. There you will edit the **File Pattern** and **Folder Pattern** fields:

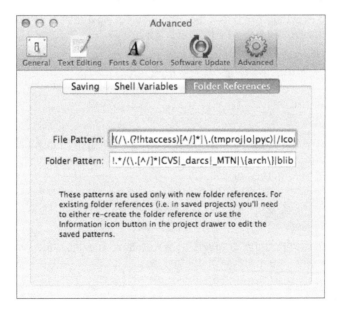

Taking the example I gave previously regarding excluding any files with the extension `.log`, the **File Pattern** field would look as follows:

```
!(/\.(?!htaccess)[^/]*|\.(tmproj|o|pyc)|/Icon\r|/svn-commit(\.[2-
9])?\.tmp|\.log)$
```

Note the `|\.log` at the end. If you aren't familiar with regular expressions, note that this says to exclude files that end in `.log` (along with excluding `.htaccess`, files ending in `.tmproj`, `.o`, `.pyc`, and so on).

Utilizing tabs (Must know)

This task is a run-through of the various ways to navigate tabs, mostly via keyboard shortcuts.

Getting ready

Open or create a new project with multiple files. Clicking on any of the files in the **Project Drawer** will open those files in new tabs.

How to do it...

- Navigate to **Next File Tab**: From the menu, select **Navigation | Next File Tab** (*Command + }* or *Command + Option* + right arrow)
- Navigate to **Previous Tab**: From the menu, select **Navigation | Previous Tab** (*Command + {* or *Command + Option* + left arrow)
- **Go to Tab**: From the menu, select **Navigation | Go to Tab** (or *Command + 1* through *Command + 9*, with the tabs ordered from left to right)

How it works...

Navigating through the tabs with the keyboard shortcuts will speed up your editing time. Once you learn these shortcuts, you can quickly go back and forth between two (or three, or four, or more) files you need to reference or edit.

There's more...

Organizing your tabs is important for an efficient workflow. This includes moving tabs around, closing tabs, and viewing the overflow of opened tabs.

Moving tabs

You can move between tabs very easily by clicking and holding the mouse cursor on the tab and dragging it to a new location.

Closing tabs

Closing tabs is as easy as clicking the *X* on the tab or using the keyboard shortcut *Command + W*. You can also use the File menu; select **File | Close Tab**.

Showing other open tabs

When you have more tabs open than the document window can show, you'll notice some double-right arrows. Clicking on these will drop down a menu with the rest of the open tabs, as shown in the following screenshot:

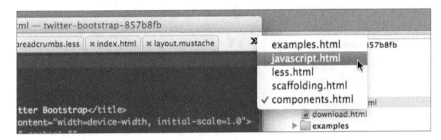

If you navigate through the tabs using **Next File Tab** (*Command + }* or *Command + Option + right arrow*) and **Previous Tab** (*Command + {* or *Command + Option + left arrow*), you will navigate to the unseen tabs as well.

Traversing files (Should know)

This task will teach you how to quickly and easily open files within a project without reaching for the mouse.

Getting ready

Open or create a project with multiple files.

How to do it...

You may navigate to files within your project in two main ways:

▶ The **Project Drawer** menu: This is the most obvious way to select a file to open. Once clicked, the file will open a new tab in the document window.

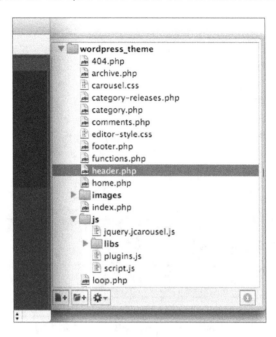

▶ The **Go to File...** option: From the menu, select **Navigation | Go To File...** (*Command + T*).

How it works...

The **Project Drawer** menu should be self-explanatory as it's simply a list of the files and folders in a project.

If you already know the name of the file you want to open, the **Go To File...** (*Command + T*) option saves a great amount of time. When you use this option, a pop-up box will appear with a list of the files in the project, as shown in the following screenshot:

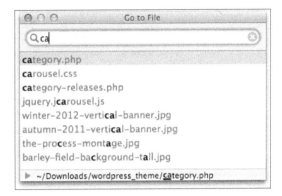

Start typing to filter the files by what you enter in the search box. Press *Tab* and then the up or down arrow to navigate your selection to the file you wish to open. Press *Enter* or *Return* to open the file in the document window and close the **Go to File...** pop-up box.

There's more...

You can toggle the **Project Drawer** at any time as well as specify which file extensions you want to open in TextMate.

Show/Hide Project Drawer

From the menu, select **View | Show/Hide Project Drawer** (*Command + Option + Control + D*).

The **Project Drawer** will attempt to open on the left-hand side by default. However, if there's no room, it will open on the right side. TextMate will remember which side it last opened on. So, in a scenario where **Project Drawer** opened on the right-hand side, was hidden, and then reopened with enough room on both sides, it will open on the right-hand side again.

Treating files as binary

When you open projects, unless you exclude certain files, TextMate will also pull in any images or executables. Though you may not mean to, you can open these files in the document window.

If you'd rather not have TextMate read these files when you click on them (usually by accident), then you can right-click on the files in the **Project Drawer** and select **Treat Files with ".xxx" Extension as Binary**. An example of this is shown in the following screenshot:

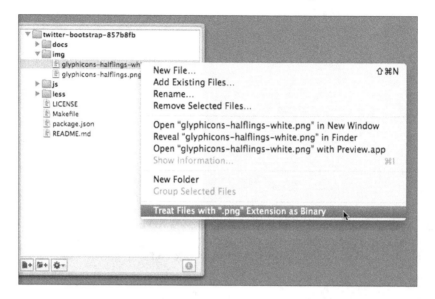

You can undo this by right-clicking on the file and selecting **Treat Files with ".xxx" Extension as Text**.

Finding text in a project (Must know)

This task describes another way to find text, this time searching through your entire project. This task will also include some tips on how to speed up your search and even cover some caveats for larger projects.

Getting ready

Open or create a project with multiple files.

How to do it...

To pull up the **Find in Project** dialog window, from the menu, select **Edit** | **Find** | **Find in Project...** (*Command + Shift + F*).

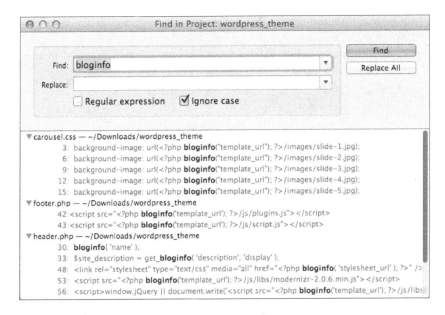

How it works...

The **Find** function works in very much the same way as **Find in a File** (*Command* + *F*). However, it will return the locations of all of the occurrences of your find in every file of your project, except for the binary files.

> ► Go to occurrence: If you'd like to open the file and go to the occurrence of the find, just click on the occurrence in the list as shown in the following screenshot:

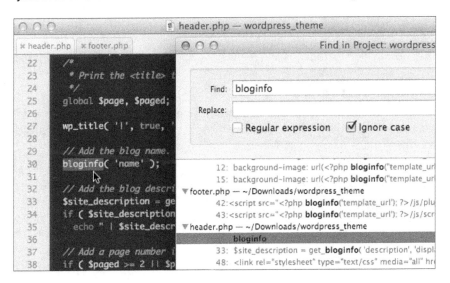

▸ The **Replace Selected** option: This option will only replace the occurrences of the find with the replace string for the current selection of occurrences. You can select multiple occurrences by holding down the *Shift* or *Command* keys while selecting. This is shown in the following screenshot:

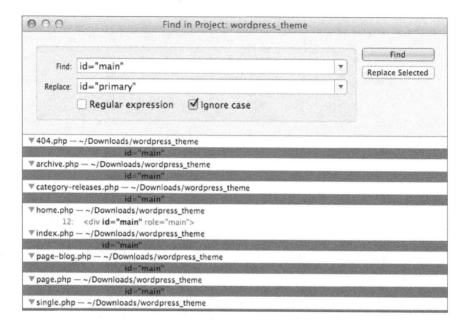

▸ **The Replace All option**: As expected, this will replace all of the occurrences of the find with the replace string regardless of what files are selected.

There's more...

Let's look at how to hide extraneous find results and speed up searching in large projects.

Hiding find occurrences

If you get a lot of results back and want to hide some occurrences to make it easier to replace selected occurrences, you can fold or collapse those results by clicking on the triangle next to the file, as shown in the following screenshot:

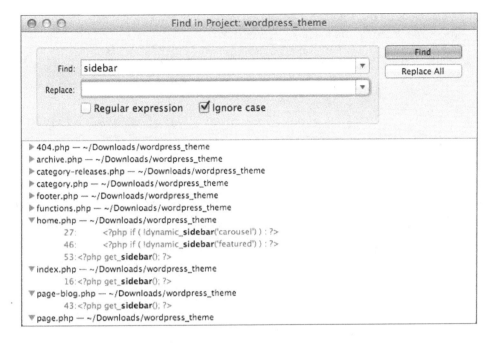

Tips to speed up searching

As mentioned in the *Creating projects* section, you can speed up searches by excluding files from your project. One method to do this is to create a new project with only the files you wish to search (for example, a particular folder or group of folders). The steps to implement for faster searching are as follows:

1. Select the folders and/or files you wish to search in **Project Drawer**.
2. Create a new project (*Command + Control + N*).

3. Drag-and-drop the selected files and/or folders into the new project's **Project Drawer** menu, as shown in the following screenshot:

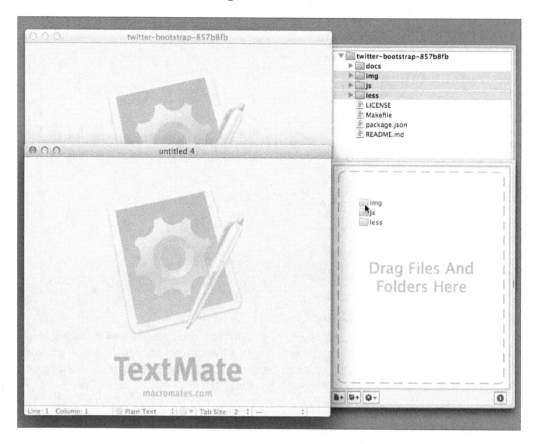

4. Perform a **Find in Project** (*Control* + *Shift* + *F*) action on the new project, as shown in the following screenshot:

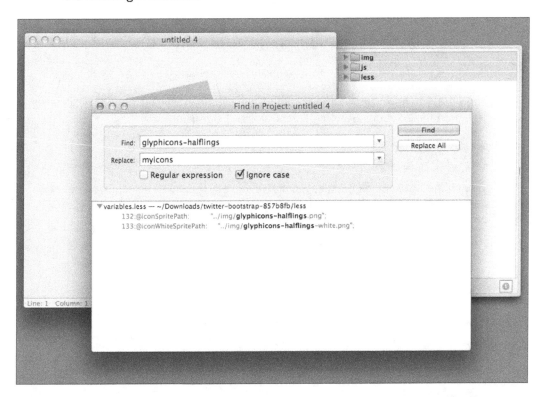

Installing bundles with GetBundles (Must know)

Installing bundles can be a bit daunting if you're not used to working in the Terminal. This task will cover finding and installing bundles with **GetBundles**, which is a bundle that allows you to install other publicly available bundles.

Getting ready

Installing GetBundles is much like installing bundles manually, which we will go over later in this task. It's more complicated than installing themes and requires you to use the Terminal application. The steps to install are as follows:

1. Open the Terminal application, which is located in your `Applications` folder under the `Utilities` folder.

2. From the Terminal, enter the following commands:

```
mkdir -p ~/Library/Application\ Support/TextMate/Bundles

cd ~/Library/Application\ Support/TextMate/Bundles

svn co http://svn.textmate.org/trunk/Review/Bundles/GetBundles.
tmbundle/

osascript -e 'tell app "TextMate" to reload bundles'
```

3. Now that you have **GetBundles** installed, you can open the **GetBundles** window via the menu by selecting **Bundles | GetBundles | Get Bundles**.

How to do it...

Once you open the **GetBundles** bundle, you can install any bundle by selecting one or more bundles and clicking the **Install Bundles** button:

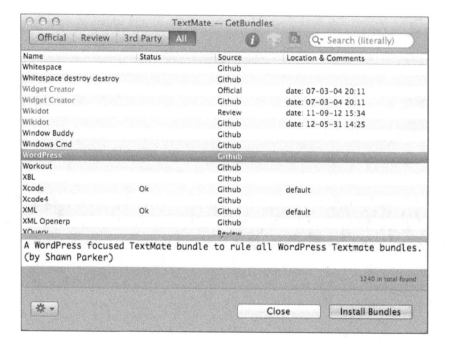

How it works...

The **GetBundles** bundle has a simple interface that lists bundles and their descriptions with the search option, filters, and tools:

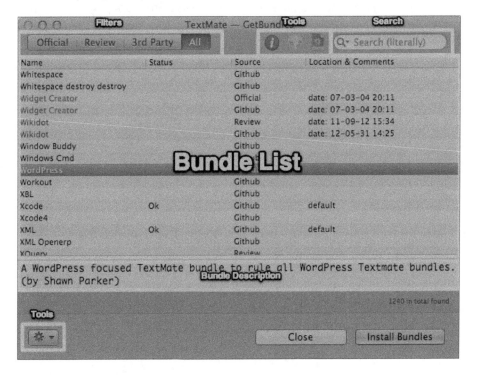

Some of the features of **GetBundles** are explained in the following section:

- ▶ Filtering: This allows you to filter the bundles by **Official**, **Under Review** (as in under review by Macromates), **3rd Party**, and **All**.

- ▶ Searching: You can search for a bundle using two methods—literal or with a regular expression. The search will apply to the current filter you have selected. It will also search both the bundle name and the description.

▸ Tools: The tools drop-down menu (that is, the gear icon in the bottom left-hand side of the window) will allow you to use options such as **Reload Bundles List**, **Refresh Local Bundle List**, **Install all Updates** for your currently installed bundles, view the log, and more. You can also see information about the bundle, show the currently installed bundles in **Finder**, and open the bundle source in Textmate with the icon tools located at the top of the **GetBundles** window. The tools drop-down menu options are shown in the following screenshot:

▸ Installed bundles: All properly installed bundles have a status of **Ok**.

▸ Sorting: All the columns in the bundle list are sortable. For example, if you want to sort by installed bundles, click on the **Status** column header until the arrow is pointed down, as shown in the following screenshot:

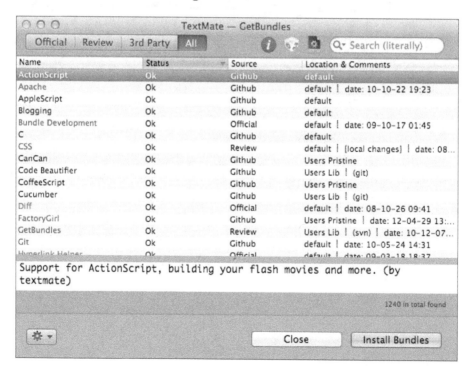

- Uninstalling bundles: Removing bundles is as easy as selecting an installed bundle and clicking the **Delete** button, which is shown in the following screenshot:

There's more...

If you'd like to install bundles manually, you can check out the source files directly from Macromate's subversion repository.

Installing bundles via Github or SVN

If you're comfortable using the Terminal, you can manually install bundles using **subversion** (**SVN**) or **git** (via **Github**):

- **Subversion** (**SVN**): The official TextMate bundles can be found in an SVN repository hosted by Macromates at `http://svn.textmate.org/trunk/`.

- **Git**: The official TextMate bundles are mirrored on Github at `https://github.com/textmate/`. TextMate bundles are typically listed in Github. Since it's a common convention, search the site for repositories with `tmbundle` in the name.

Learning and loving bundles (Must know)

This task will quickly cover the use of bundles, including the beauty of tab completions and how to easily find the bundle item you're looking for along with the tab completion abbreviation or the keyboard shortcut.

How to do it...

- Tab completion: Type in a tab trigger, for example, `div` in an HTML document, and press the *Tab* key. The following screenshot shows how the code is auto-completed:

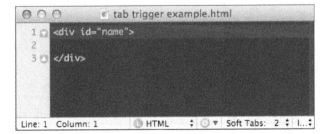

- Opening bundle actions: You can open the bundle actions by clicking on the gear icon in the status menu or with the keyboard shortcut *Control + Escape*.

- The **Select Bundle Item** window: This window allows you to quickly find a particular bundle action, whether it's a tab-completed snippet or a keyboard shortcut. You can open the window from the menu by selecting **Bundles | Select Bundle Item...** or use the keyboard shortcut *Command + Control + T*. This window is shown in the following screenshot:

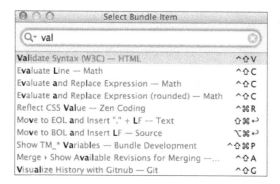

How it works...

- Tab completion is one of many ways in which bundles can help with writing and code development. They are very useful shortcuts that will greatly speed up your coding.

- Opening bundle actions is just like opening the bundles menu item, but with the benefit of easier access through a simple keyboard shortcut.

- The **Select Bundle Item** window is used just like the **Go to File...** option with projects. You can type in the search bar to quickly filter all of the bundle actions.

There's more...

If you want to dig deeper into learning more about a particular bundle, **Bundle Editor** is the place to go.

Exploring bundles

You can filter and view many other bundle items, such as commands and macros, in the
Bundle Editor (select **Bundles | Bundle Editor | Show Bundle Editor** or *Command + Option
+ Control + B*). If you want to know how a particular bundle item works, find it here. The
Bundle Editor window is shown in the following screenshot:

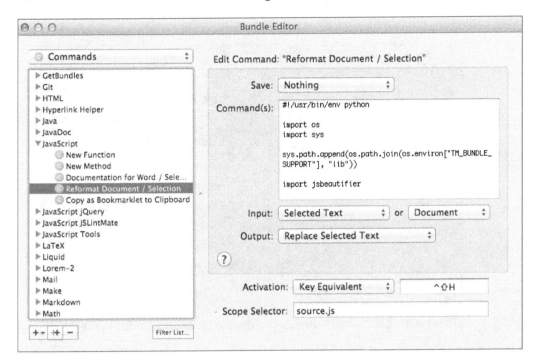

Making a TODO list (Should know)

This task will utilize the official TextMate **TODO** bundle to display a to-do list compiled
directly from your project using common comment keywords such as TODO, FIXME,
CHANGED, and RADAR.

How to do it...

▸ Insert a **TODO** item by typing a TODO, FIXME, CHANGED, or RADAR keyword anywhere in the comments of your document. You may also use tab completion by typing todo and then pressing *Tab*, which will automatically create a new comment. The different types of comments are shown in the following screenshot:

```
●○○                               script.js
217    // FIXME: Doesn't work anymore
218    $('.banner-container').find('.customize-button').hide();
219
220    // CHANGED: Instead of floats, we're specifying cell width
221    $('.banner-container:nth-child(3n+1)').addClass("cell-1");
222    $('.banner-container:nth-child(3n+2)').addClass("cell-2");
223    $('.banner-container:nth-child(3n+3)').addClass("cell-3");
224
225    /*
226        TODO: move to top of the function
227    */
228    var bannerContainers = $('.banner-container'),
229        numBannerContainers = $('.banner-container').length,
230        lastCell= 0;
231
232    // Calculate out last cell
233    // TODO: Change to nth-child like above
234    if ((numBannerContainers % 3) === 0) {
235        lastCell = numBannerContainers - 4;   // index of 0
236    } else {
237        lastCell = (Math.floor(numBannerContainers / 3) * 3) - 1;
238    }
239    $('.banner-container:gt('+lastCell+')').addClass('last');
240
Line: 217  Column: 35     JavaScript          ⊘ ▾  Soft Tabs:  4   init
```

▸ You can view the **TODO** list for the current document through the menu by selecting **Bundles | TODO | Show TODO List** or via the keyboard shortcut *Control + Shift + T*. The list is shown in the following screenshot:

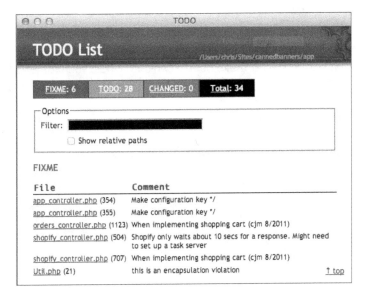

How it works...

As you may have surmised, the **TODO** bundle will search through your current document or project for the **TODO**, **FixMe**, **changed**, and **RADAR** keywords. Note that the keyword is not case sensitive and can be followed by a whitespace character, a comma, or a colon. This is shown in the following screenshot:

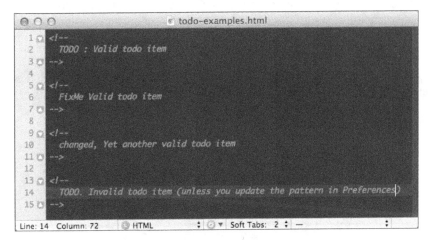

To search through multiple files or folders in your project, you need to select those files and/or folders in the **Project Drawer** menu. For example, to search the entire project select the top-level folder and click on **Show TODO List** (*Control + Shift + T*).

There's more...

You may customize the **TODO** bundle to suit your color and pattern preferences as well as add more markers. We'll also cover the **Tasks** bundle, which will help you create well-formatted to-do lists.

Setting other preferences

You can choose what words count as **TODO** keywords. To do this, go to **TODO Preferences** via the File menu by selecting **Bundles | TODO | Preferences**. This window is shown in the following screenshot:

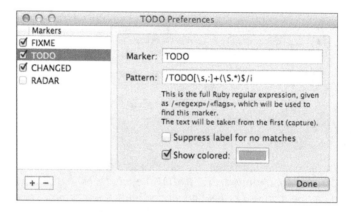

You may also change the color and regular expression pattern of the keywords, making this bundle quite versatile.

Tasks bundle

If you love to-do lists, a similar bundle called Tasks is also available for installation via **GetBundles**. The Tasks bundle allows you to easily create simple to-do items (*Ins* or *fn + return* on laptops to create a task) and mark them as complete (*Command + D*). An example of a to-do list is shown in the following screenshot:

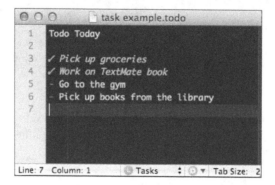

More information on official TextMate bundles

The other official TextMate bundles are extremely helpful. However, this book will attempt to show you bundles and tools about which you might not already be aware. You can read about some highlights of the other bundles in the TextMate manual at `http://manual.macromates.com/en/bundles`.

Becoming a Zen Coding master (Should know)

Zen Coding is a method to code HTML at top speed through the use of CSS selectors and other abbreviations. This task will briefly cover the philosophy and use of the most common bundle items.

Getting ready

Install the Zen Coding bundle via GetBundles.

How to do it...

In order to expand a Zen Coding abbreviation or alias, you need to use the keyboard shortcut *Command + E*, or from the menu select **Bundles | Zen Coding | Expand Abbreviation**.

For example, **div#main** will expand to **<div id="main"></div>**

Here are some more examples:

How it works...

On the Zen Coding website, at `http://code.google.com/p/zen-coding/`, Zen Coding is defined as an editor plugin for high-speed HTML, XML, and XSL (or any other structured code format) coding and editing. The core of this plugin is a powerful abbreviation engine, which allows you to expand expressions—similar to CSS selectors—into HTML code.

Zen Coding can greatly expedite HTML development. There are some other helpful actions included in this bundle:

- ▸ The **Increment/Decrement number by 1** action (*Command + ?*): Add or subtract 1 from the number to the left of the cursor. An example use case would be if you duplicate a line (*Control + Shift + D*) and then want to increase the ID by 1.
- ▸ The **Remove Tag** action (*Command + Shift + K*): Remove the tag surrounding the text.
- ▸ The **Wrap with Abbreviation** action (*Command + Shift + A*): Wrap current selection with the abbreviation you enter into the pop-up dialog after running this action.

There are more actions, so definitely explore all of them. A handy cheat sheet is available at `http://code.google.com/p/zen-coding/wiki/CheatSheets`.

There's more...

The purpose of covering Zen Coding in this book is to highlight the power of TextMate as a full-featured coding tool. It will save you a lot of time if you do a lot of HTML and CSS coding.

More information about Zen Coding

To find out more information about Zen Coding, the philosophy, and more actions, you should visit the official website at `http://code.google.com/p/zen-coding/`. Listed at this website are a number of plugins available for other applications, should your friends and colleagues be jealous of your fast HTML coding abilities.

Zen CSS

Along the same lines as Zen Coding for HTML, there is also Zen Coding for CSS, which mostly utilizes short-form abbreviations for CSS properties.

Find out more by going to this wiki page at `http://code.google.com/p/zen-coding/wiki/ZenCSSPropertiesEn`.

Blogging more efficiently (Should know)

With the popularity of **WordPress** and other **Content Management Systems** (**CMS**) that incorporate **What You See Is What You Get** (**WYSIWYG**) editors, such as **TinyMCE** and auto-saving, writing in separate editors seems a bit unnecessary or "old school". However, I still often prefer to work remotely, which sometimes means no Internet and makes TextMate a perfect offline utility. This task will cover a few of the more useful blogging bundles: **Blogging** and **Hyperlink Helper**.

Getting ready

Install the Blogging and Hyperlink Helper bundles via GetBundles.

How to do it...

The **Hyperlink Helper** option:

▶ The **Wrap selection with link** option: Wrap a hyperlink tag no matter what kind of document you're in (HTML, Markdown, Textile, and so on) by using *Control + Shift + L* or from the menu by selecting **Bundles | Hyperlink Helper | Wrap selection as link**.

▶ Search for selection and wrap with link: Use the keyboard shortcut *Command + Control + Shift + L* (or select **Bundles | Hyperlink Helper | Lookup word on Google and link**) to search for the selected text and wrap that text with the first result from Google.

The **Blogging** option:

1. The **Setup** option: First you must define your list of blogs by entering the blog name and **XML-RPC** (that is, **Remote Procedure Call** using XML) URL. From the menu select **Bundles | Blogging | Setup**. This is shown in the following screenshot:

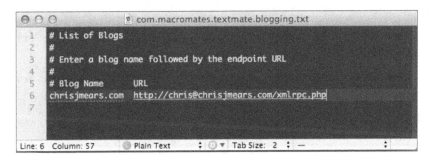

2. Fetching blogs: In order to start editing blog posts, you'll need to fetch a list of the blog entries. From the menu select **Bundles | Blogging | Fetch Post**. The **Fetch Post** window is shown in the next screenshot.

3. The most common XML-RPC locations are as follows:

    ❏ **Moveable Type**: `http://username@myblogdomain.com/mt-xmlrpc.cgi#1`

    ❏ **WordPress**: `http://username@myblogdomain.com/xmlrpc.php`

    ❏ **Typo**: `http://username@myblogdomain.com/backend/xmlrpc`

4. Edit and save the blog: Edit the blog entry in Markdown (see the *Markdown and Textile* section later in this chapter) and save blog as you normally would (*Command + S*). Once you're done editing, post to the blog with the keyboard shortcut *Command + Control + P* (or select **Bundles | Blogging | Post to Blog**).

How it works...

The **Hyperlink Helper** option is quite useful when you want to quickly insert references into your documents without having to go back and forth between your browser, search for the address, and then paste it into your document.

It also has some further functionality, such as searching for word definition links in Wikipedia and more advanced Yahoo! search engine searches.

The **Help** documentation for the **Blogging** bundle is quite helpful, so you should read it if you have any issues. From the menu select **Bundles | Blogging | Help**.

Markdown and Textile (Should know)

Markdown and Textile are plain text file formats that can easily be converted to HTML (and other formats) through the use of easily accessible libraries. This task will cover both formats and explain why you may want to use one over the other depending on your project.

Getting ready

Install the Markdown and Textile Bundles via GetBundles.

How to do it...

It's as simple as selecting the file format from the document status menu. The following screenshot is an example of using the Markdown bundle:

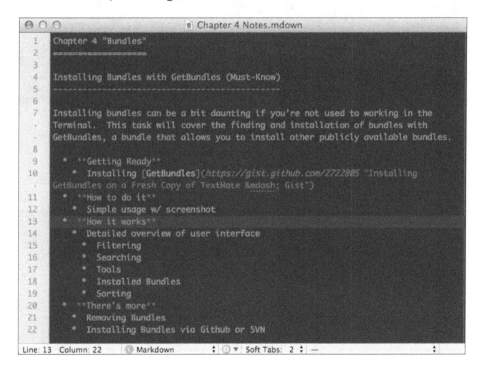

The following screenshot is an example of using the Textile bundle:

```
 ● ○ ○                              Chapter 4 Notes.textile
 1    h1. Chapter 4 "Bundles"
 2
 3    h2. Installing Bundles with GetBundles (Must-Know)
 4
 5    #  Installing bundles can be a bit daunting if you're not used to working in the
      Terminal.  This task will cover the finding and installation of bundles with
      GetBundles, a bundle that allows you to install other publicly available bundles.
 6    #  _Getting Ready_
 7    **   Installing GetBundles
 8    #  _How to do it_
 9    **   Simple usage w/ screenshot
10    #  _How it works_
11    ** Detailed overview of user interface
12    *** Filtering
13    *** Searching
14    *** Tools
15    ***   Installed Bundles
16    ***   Sorting
17    #  _There's more_
18    **   Removing Bundles
19    **   Installing Bundles via Github or SVN

 Line: 14   Column: 1        Textile           ⇕ ⊙ ▼  Soft Tabs:  2 ⇕    Installing Bundles with GetB... ⇕
```

How it works...

Though both the Markdown and Textile bundles make it easier to utilize these lightweight markup languages, the real power lies within the syntax. Both bundles provide easy access to the documentation with the keyboard shortcut *Control + H*. The following screenshot is an example of the **Markdown** documentation:

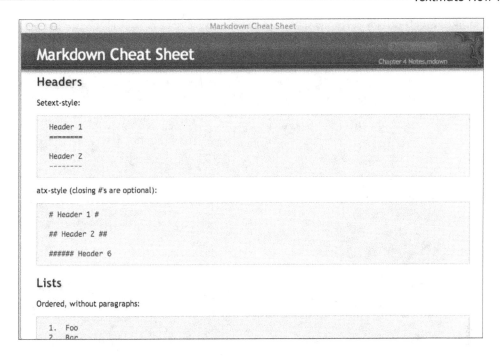

The following screenshot is an example of the **Textile** documentation:

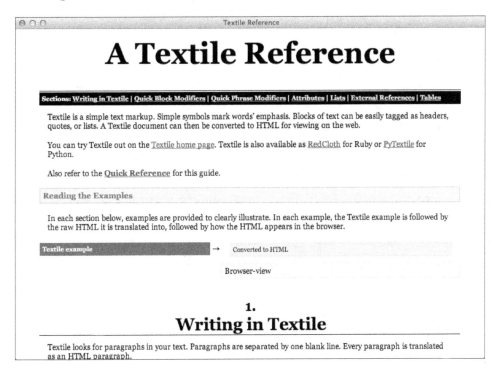

With Markdown, if you are currently making edits, you may instead see a tooltip with helpful instructions to speed up your editing. This is shown in the following screenshot:

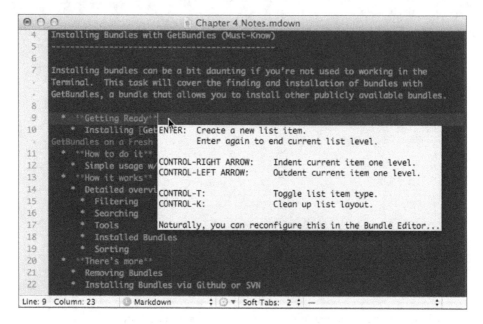

You can find out more about these formats and their syntaxes at the following sites:

For Markdown use `http://daringfireball.net/projects/markdown/`, and for Textile use `http://redcloth.org/hobix.com/textile/`.

There's more...

You may be asking yourself, "Should I use Textile or Markdown?" The answer to this question largely depends on the project at hand.

Which should I use?

Developed by John Gruber and Aaron Swartz, Markdown was meant to allow a format that is easy to write, read, and convertible into a structured format such as HTML.

Textile is similar in nature but focuses more on marking up the language. Originally developed by Dean Allen, it is regarded as a "humane web text generator".

History aside, it really comes down to your particular needs. I typically use Textile when I want greater control over the markup's end result. Textile is also used for a lot of wikis and blogs. I use Markdown whenever I want to format plain text in a pretty way and want the document to be easily convertible into HTML (for example, my resume or notes). They can both do about the same amount things, so it's purely up to you.

Using macros (Should know)

Macros make it easy to record several actions or keystrokes and then replay them multiple times. This task will provide an overview of how to record and subsequently execute macros in your document.

How to do it...

1. You can start (and stop) a macro recording by using the keyboard shortcut *Command + Option + M* (or select **Bundles | Macro | Start Recording/Stop Macro**). Once enabled, you will notice a red recording dot in the bottom-right corner of the document window, as shown in the following screenshot:

2. Once you've stopped recording (*Option + Command + M*), you can save the macro by using the keyboard shortcut *Control + Command + M* (or select **Bundles | Macro | Save Last Recording**), which will open the **Bundle Editor** window. Enter a name for the macro and choose an activation method of either a keyboard shortcut or tab trigger, as shown in the following screenshot:

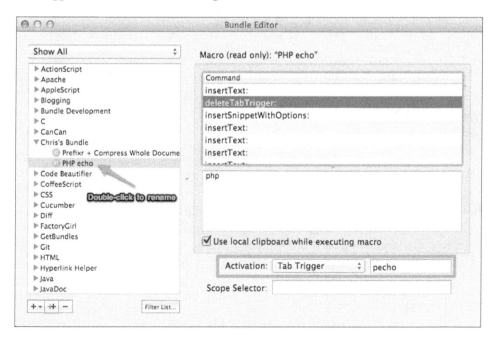

3. Once named and set up with an activation method, you can use your newly created macro! The following screenshot shows a macro being used in PHP:

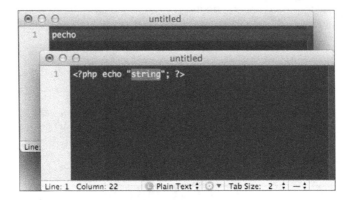

How it works...

Macros are best used for keystrokes that you keep repeating. In the previous example, I made a macro out of a common pattern I use in PHP development (WordPress, CakePHP, and so on) to print out a string, which typically includes a variable (for example, for debugging purposes).

Temporary macros

If you just want to use your macro without saving it long-term, you can use the previously recorded macro by hitting the keyboard shortcut *Shift + Command + M*, or from the menu by selecting **Bundles | Macros | Replay Last Recording**.

 Your temporary macro will be lost if you record another macro or close TextMate.

There's more...

Editing your macro requires a little bit of XML knowledge, but it is easily done using TextMate to open the bundle source files.

Editing macros

Sometimes it can be difficult to record a macro perfectly the first time. The bad news is that TextMate doesn't currently support editing macros. The good news is that if you're comfortable with XML, you can edit the `.plist` file by opening it in TextMate. The steps for editing macros are as follows:

1. Open a file (*Command + O*).

2. Select the **Show Hidden Files** checkbox as shown in the following screenshot:

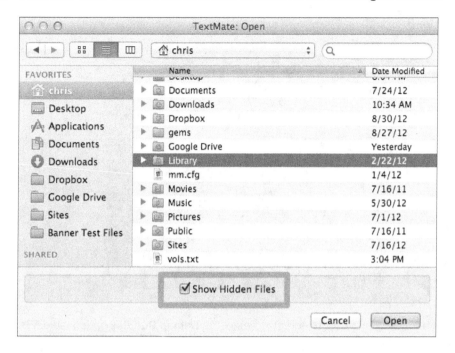

3. Navigate to your `Home` folder, then `Library/Application Support/TextMate/`
   `Bundles`, then select the bundle name and click on **Open**, as shown in the
   following screenshot:

4. The `.tmbundle` file will open as a project. You will find your macros in the **Macros** folder, as shown in the following screenshot:

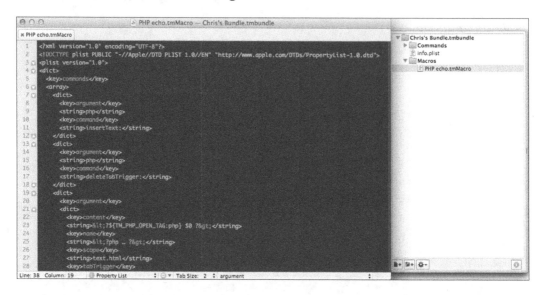

Once you edit your bundle, don't forget to select the **Reload Bundles** option (select **Bundles | Bundle Editor | Reload Bundles**).

Executing shell commands (Become an expert)

This task will cover how to execute shell commands directly from the current document.

How to do it...

The steps to execute shell commands directly from the current document are as follows:

1. Add a new command into the **Bundle Editor** window (*Control + Option + Command + B*) by clicking on the plus (**+**) icon and selecting **New Command**:

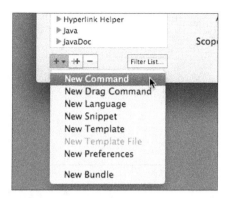

2. Fill in the **Command(s)** text field with the commands you wish to execute, along with the **Input**, **Output**, and **Activation** options. You can also select this option via the **Bundles** menu.

3. For the **Command(s)** text field, enter **curl -sSd "css=$TM_SELECTED_TEXT" \http://prefixr.com/api/index.php** for the **Input** option, set **Selected Text or Document**; for the **Output** option, set **Replace Selected Text**; and for the **Activation** option, set **Key Equivalent** and *Control + Option + Command + U*, as shown in the following screenshot:

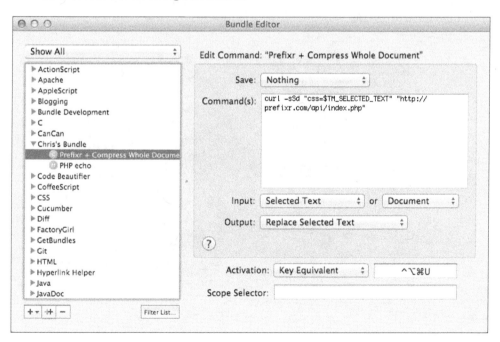

4. Execute the command by selecting the text you wish to input. This is shown in the following screenshot:

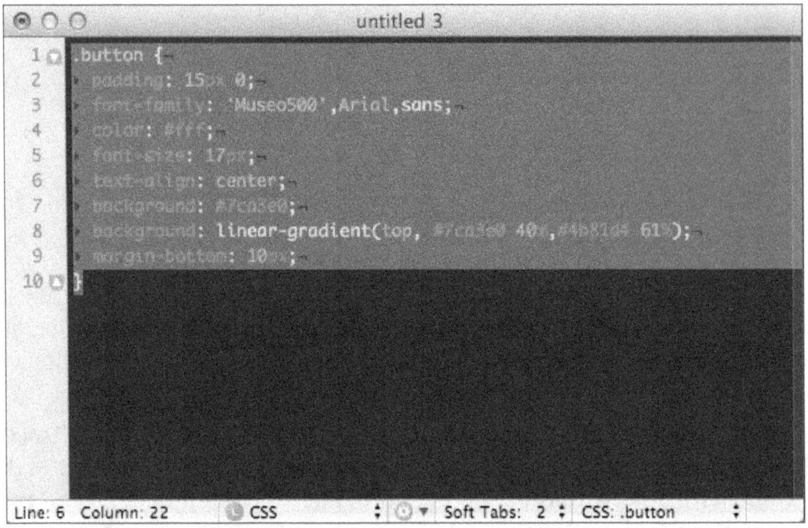

5. And then use the chosen activation action (the keyboard shortcut *Control + Option + Command + U* in this example):

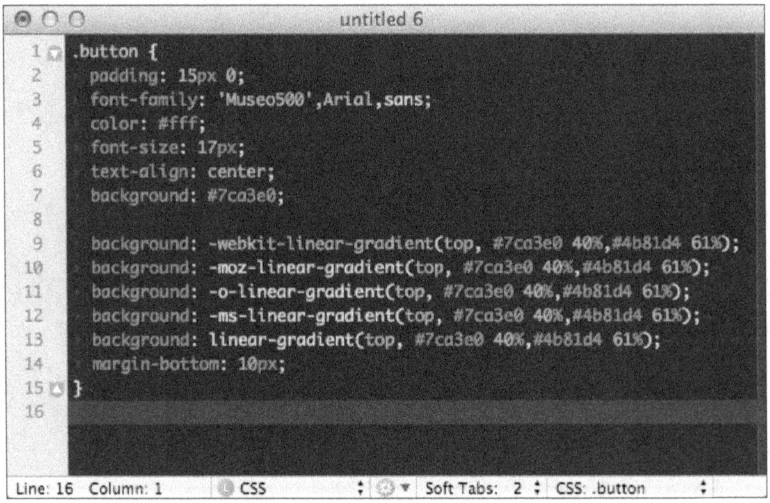

How it works...

The example in this task uses Jeffery Way's **Prefixr** (http://www.prefixr.com/), which is a fantastic utility to make the CSS cross-browser compatible quickly and easily.

From the previous example, when you use the keyboard shortcut, the selected text (the input) will be sent to Prefixr via cURL (http://curl.haxx.se/), which is a command-line utility that transfers data from a variety of protocols, such as HTTP. The returned data (the output) will then replace the selected text.

There's more...

Let's also look at how to execute commands from the document editor. Plus, we'll find out how to set environment variables to aid in development.

Executing lines and inserting results

Another way to execute commands in TextMate is to execute the current line and return the results. This can be done from the menu (select **Text | Execute Selection Inserting Result**) or the keyboard shortcut *Control + R*:

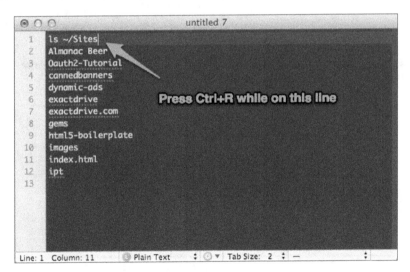

More on environment variables

In this section's example, we made use of the TextMate environment variable **$TM_ SELECTED_TEXT**. There are a number of other similar environment variables that can be used for commands and more complex bundle operations. A full list of the variables can be found on Macromate's TextMate wiki:

http://manual.macromates.com/en/environment_variables.html

You may also wish to utilize static shell variables (select **Preferences | Advanced | Shell Variables**), which you can use to declare usernames and passwords to your MySQL database or services such as **Shopify** (http://www.shopify.com/). The **Shell Variables** window is shown in the following screenshot:

You can also specify shell variables at the project level by clicking on the information icon in the **Project Drawer** menu, as shown in the following screenshot:

The **Project Information** window is shown in the following screenshot, where usernames and passwords of services such as MySQL can be set:

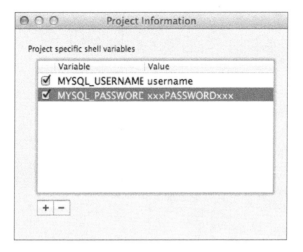

Thank you for buying
TextMate How-To

About Packt Publishing

Packt, pronounced 'packed', published its first book "*Mastering phpMyAdmin for Effective MySQL Management*" in April 2004 and subsequently continued to specialize in publishing highly focused books on specific technologies and solutions.

Our books and publications share the experiences of your fellow IT professionals in adapting and customizing today's systems, applications, and frameworks. Our solution based books give you the knowledge and power to customize the software and technologies you're using to get the job done. Packt books are more specific and less general than the IT books you have seen in the past. Our unique business model allows us to bring you more focused information, giving you more of what you need to know, and less of what you don't.

Packt is a modern, yet unique publishing company, which focuses on producing quality, cutting-edge books for communities of developers, administrators, and newbies alike. For more information, please visit our website: www.packtpub.com.

Writing for Packt

We welcome all inquiries from people who are interested in authoring. Book proposals should be sent to author@packtpub.com. If your book idea is still at an early stage and you would like to discuss it first before writing a formal book proposal, contact us; one of our commissioning editors will get in touch with you.

We're not just looking for published authors; if you have strong technical skills but no writing experience, our experienced editors can help you develop a writing career, or simply get some additional reward for your expertise.

Sencha Touch Hotshot

ISBN: 978-1-84951-890-1   Paperback: 327 pages

Learn to use the Sencha Touch programmimg language and expand your skills by building 10 unique applications

1. Learn the Sencha Touch programming language by building real, working applications

2. Each chapter focuses on different features and programming approaches; you can decide which is right for you

3. Full of well-explained example code and rich with screenshots

UDK iOS Game Development Beginner's Guide

ISBN: 978-1-84969-190-1   Paperback: 280 pages

Create your own third-person shooter game using the Unreal development Kit to create your own game on Apple's iOS devices, such as the iPhone. iPad, and iPod Touch

1. Learn the fundamentals of the Unreal Editor to create gameplay environments and interactive elements

2. Create a third person shooter intended for the iOS and optimize any game with special considerations for the target platform

3. Take your completed game to Apple's App Store with a detailed walkthrough on how to do it

Please check **www.PacktPub.com** for information on our titles

www.ingramcontent.com/pod-product-compliance
Lightning Source LLC
LaVergne TN
LVHW080104070326
832902LV00014B/2410